My First Book about the Alphabet of Marsupials (Kangaroos, Koalas, & More)

Amazing Animal Books Children's Picture Books

By Molly Davidson

Mendon Cottage Books

JD-Biz Publishing

Read More Amazing Animal Books

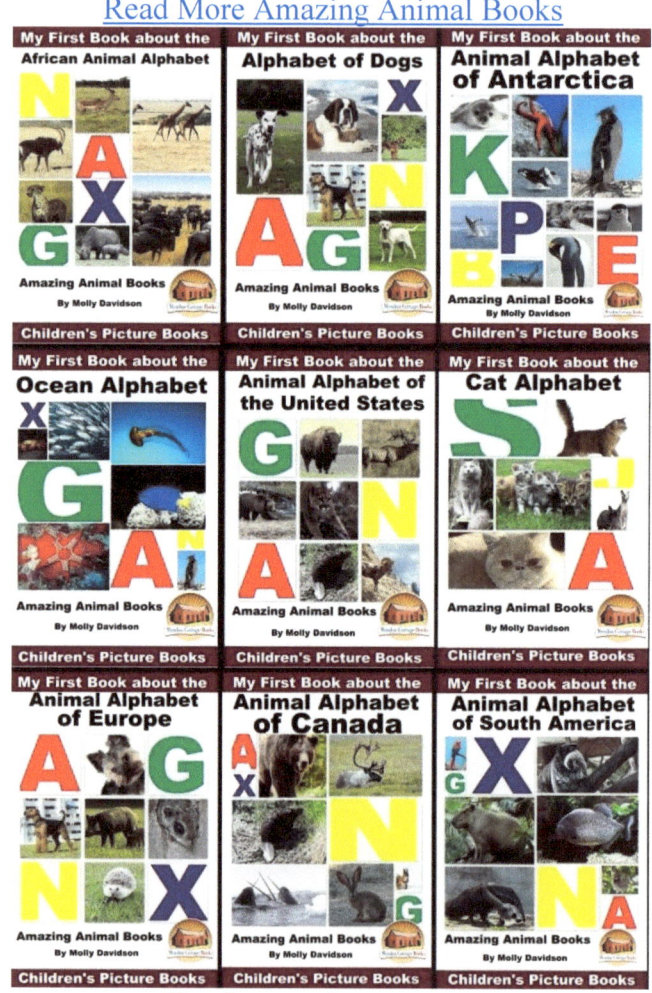

Purchase at Amazon.com

Download Free Books!
http://MendonCottageBooks.com

Introduction

Marsupials are animals that have a pouch on the mother's belly, where she keeps her babies until they are developed.

Most marsupials are found in Australia and New Guinea.

 is for an Antechinus.

Antechinus live in the tropical rainforests of Australia and New Guinea.

The boys only mate once, which uses most of their energy and they usually die after.

 is for a Bandicoot.

Bertram Lobert © <u>Wikimedia Commons</u>

Banicoots look like a rat, but are actually closely related to rabbits.

They are nocturnal, which means active at night, and live in the forests of Australia.

 **is for a Colocolo Opossum.**

Eliminate123 © <u>Wikimedia Commons</u>

Colocolo opossums are also called monito del monte, which is Spanish for "little mountain monkey."

They are nocturnal, and live in the bamboo of the Andes Mountains in South America.

D is for a Dasyurus, the scientific name for a Quoll.

Quoll are a nocturnal (active at night) marsupial cat, native to Australia, New Guinea, and Tasmania.

Babies will live in their mothers pouch until they are about 6 months old.

E is for an Elegant Fat-Tailed Mouse Opossum.

Yamil Hussein E. © Wikimedia Commons

Elegant Fat-Tailed Mouse Opossums get their name because they store fat in their tail which makes it larger than most opossums.

They live in Chile, and the mothers can have up to 15 babies eating in her pouch at one time.

 **is for a Feathertail Glider.**

Found in Australia, the feathertail glider is the smallest gliding mammal in the World.

Their body measures about 3 inches long.

They spend most of their time almost 50 feet up in Eucalyptus trees.

G is for a Greater Bilby.

The greater bilby is a nocturnal, rabbit sized marsupial, found in Australia.

On the second Sunday in September, is National Bilby Day in Australia, where money is raised to help keep them from extinction.

 **is for a Joey.**

Joey is the name of a baby marsupial.

They are born after about 4 weeks inside their mother; they are about the size of a jellybean.

Next they crawl inside their mother's pouch to finish developing, for about 6 months.

K is for a Koala.

Koalas spend most of their day sleeping in Eucalyptus trees found in Australia, and spend the cool nights eating the leaves of the tree.

L is for a Leadbeater's Possum.

Tirin © Wikimedia Commons

Leadbeater's possums are critically endangered and can only be found in the forests of Victoria, Australia.

They are nocturnal, and live high up in some of the World's tallest trees.

 is for a **Musky Rat - Kangaroo.**

PanBK © <u>Wikimedia Commons</u>

Musky rat - kangaroos are only found in the northeast rainforests of Australia.

They have scales on their feet and tail.

They eat fruit and large seeds that have fallen from the trees.

 is also for a Marsupial Mole.

Lydekker, Richard © <u>Wikimedia Commons</u>

Marsupial moles are very rare; they are also blind and have no ears.

They live underground in burrows in the Western Australian deserts and only come to the surface after it has rained.

 is for a Numbat.

Numbat mothers do NOT have a pouch on their belly, like other marsupials; instead her babies just hold on and are kept hidden under her long fur.

They are an endangered species only found in Southern Australia.

 **is for an Opossum.**

Opossums are one of the only species of marsupials found in North America.

They eat roadkill, frogs, snakes, and worms.

They are more likely, than any other animal, to carry rabies, a disease that causes madness.

P is for a Pademelon.

Pademelons are a small marsupial related to kangaroos and wallabies, living in the forests of Australia and Tasmania.

P is also for a Potoroo.

Potoroos are an endangered marsupial, which look like a kangaroo, but is the size of a rabbit.

In the early 1800s they were very common throughout Australia, and would eat many of the farmers' crops.

 **is for a Quokka.**

Quokkas are a subspecies of the wallaby, found on the coast of Australia.

It has a short tail and legs, but can still hop through grass at up to 20 miles per hour.

R is for a Red Kanagroo.

Red kangaroos are the largest marsupials in the World, standing up to 6 feet tall.

They can hop up to 25 feet in one leap.

Red kangaroos may fight each other by kicking with their strong back legs.

S is for a Sugar Glider.

Sugar gliders have a 5 inch body, but their tail can be over 7 inches long.

Their large eyes help them see at night.

T is for a Thylacine.

Baker; E. J. Keller. © <u>Wikimedia Commons</u>

Thylacine, also called a Tasmanian tiger, became extinct in 1936.

They were the World's largest meat-eating marsupials.

Their pouch opens in the back, not in the front like other marsupials.

T is also for a Tasmanian Devil.

Tasmanian devils give birth to 20 or 30 babies, which all crawl into her pouch, but only about 4 survive because she cannot feed that many.

They are mean and known to make a high screeching sound when threatened, usually before they attack.

U is for an Ursine Tree - Kangaroo.

Ursine tree - kangaroos can only be found in the Australian rainforests.

They are able to jump 60 feet from a tree to the ground without getting hurt.

Babies stop living in their mothers' pouch when they are about 10 months old and stay with her until about 18 months old.

V

is for a Vombatidae, the scientific name for a Wombat.

Wombats live under ground, in Australia, during the day and come out at night to eat grass and tree bark.

They can live up to 26 years in the wild.

W  is for a Wallaroo.

Wallaroos are a combination of a kangaroo and a wallaby.

The boys can weigh up to 100 pounds, the girls only weigh up to about 50 pounds.

They live in the mountains of eastern Australia.

W is also for a Wallaby.

Wallabies are a smaller marsupial, which are related to the kangaroo.

Very few animals can catch a wallaby; they can hop up to 30 miles per hour, except dingoes and foxes.

 **is for a Yellow-Bellied Glider.**

Lydekker, Richard © <u>Wikimedia Commons</u>

The yellow - bellied glider lives in the Eucalyptus trees of eastern Australia.

They have a very loud growl that can be heard from over 1/3 of a mile away.

They can glide up to 500 feet and jump up to 328 feet between branches.

Conclusion

I hope you have enjoyed reading about some of the amazing animals called marsupials.

One more fact, marsupials have been on the Earth for more than 100 million years.

Horses
For Kids

Amazing Animal Books
For Young Readers
By John and
Annalee Davidson

Ponies
For Kids

Meridian Cottage Books

Amazing Animal Books
For Young Readers
Rachel Smith

Ten Amazing
Horses
For Kids

Nature Books for Kids
JD-Biz Publishing
K. Bennett

Akhal-Teke
"The Golden Horse
of the desert"
For Kids

Nature Books for Kids
JD-Biz Publishing
K. Bennett

Suffolk-Punch
"The Gentle Giant"
For Kids

Nature Books for Kids
JD-Biz Publishing
K. Bennett

Shires
"The great Horse"
For Kids

Nature Books for Kids
JD-Biz Publishing
K. Bennett

Colonial Spanish
"Horse of the Americas"
For Kids

Nature Books for Kids
JD-Biz Publishing
K. Bennett

Canadian
"The Little Iron Horse"
For Kids

Nature Books for Kids
JD-Biz Publishing
K. Bennett

Cleveland Bays
"History and Future"
Horses For Kids

Nature Books for Kids
JD-Biz Publishing
K. Bennett

Our books are available at

1. Amazon.com

2. Barnes and Noble

3. Itunes

4. Kobo

5. Smashwords

6. Google Play Books

Download Free Books!
http://MendonCottageBooks.com

Publisher

JD-Biz Corp

P O Box 374

Mendon, Utah 84325

http://www.jd-biz.com/

www.ingramcontent.com/pod-product-compliance
Lightning Source LLC
Chambersburg PA
CBHW050902290526
45792CB00002B/674